# Physical Spanish Phonics

A Sound, Action and Spelling System for Teaching Spanish Phonics

Jenny Bell
Sue Cave
Jean Haig

We hope you and your pupils enjoy the activities in this book. Brilliant Publications publishes many other books for teaching modern foreign languages. To find out more details on any of our titles please go to our website: www.brilliantpublications.co.uk.

Buena Idea
¡Es Español!
Juguemos Todos Juntos
Learn Spanish with Luis y Sofía Part 1
Learn Spanish with Luis y Sofía Part 2
Lotto Español
¡Me Gusta Cantar!
Spanish Festivals and Traditions
Spanish Pen Pals Made Easy
Spanish Speaking Activities
¡Vamos a Cantar!

Published by Brilliant Publications Limited
Unit 10,
Sparrow Hall Farm,
Edlesborough,
Dunstable,
Bedfordshire,
LU6 2ES

Website: www.brilliantpublications.co.uk

Tel: 01525 222292
Fax: 01525 222720

The name 'Brilliant Publications' and the logo are registered trade marks.

Written by Jenny Bell, Sue Cave and Jean Haig
Illustrated by Kerry Ingham
Cover illustration by Kerry Ingham and Brilliant Publications Limited
Video and audio files produced by Hart McLeod
Interactive file production by Lapiz Digital
Printed in the UK

© 2020 Jenny Bell, Sue Cave and Jean Haig (text);
   Brilliant Publications Ltd (design and layout)
Printed ISBN: 978-0-85747-805-4 (Book with CD-ROM. They are not sold separately.)

First printed and published 2020

The right of Jenny Bell, Sue Cave and Jean Haig to be identified as co-authors of this work has been asserted by themselves in accordance with the Copyright, Design and Patents Act 1988.

Pages 26–90 are photocopiable. These pages have the phrase 'This page may be photocopied by the purchasing institution only' written at the bottom of each. They may be photocopied by the purchasing institution or individual teachers for classroom use only, without permission from the publisher and without declaration to the Copyright Licensing Agency or the Publishers' Licensing Services. The material in this book may not be reproduced in any other form or for any other purpose without the prior permission of the publisher.

The CD-ROM may be used by the purchasing institution only. Purchasers may use the images in the Smart Board gallery files and Promethean flipchart files to create their own resources. Resources 1–18 on the CD-ROM may be printed out for use by the purchasing institution only.

# Contents

Preface .................................................................................................................... 5
Sounds and Accents ............................................................................................. 6
Keywords .............................................................................................................. 7
How to Become Familiar with the 20 Sounds of *Physical Spanish Phonics* ..... 8–14
The Seven Step Process for Embedding Phonics in Foreign Language Teaching ........... 15
Classroom Activities for Practising Phonics in Spanish Language Lessons ............ 16–25
Resource Sheets .............................................................................................. 26–93
    R 1 – Sounds, Actions and Spellings ................................................................. 26
    R 2 – Description of Physical Actions ........................................................... 27–31
    R 3 – International Phonetic Symbols with Images and Actions ........................ 32
    R 4 – International Phonetic Symbols with Mouth Positions ............................. 33
    R 5 – Display Cards for Sounds, Actions and Spellings ................................. 34–43
    R 6 – Flashcards for Ten Colours ................................................................ 44–45
    R 7 – Flashcards for Numbers 0–14 ............................................................ 46–48
    R 8 – Flashcards for Family ........................................................................ 49–51
    R 9 – Flashcards for Days of the Week ....................................................... 52–53
    R 10 – Flashcards for Months of the Year .................................................... 54–56
    R 11 – Match the Sounds to the Actions – Grapheme only .......................... 57–61
    R 12 – Match the Sounds to the Actions – Image and Grapheme ................ 62–66
    R 13 – Spell the Grapheme ......................................................................... 67–71
    R 14 – Colour Match Cards ........................................................................ 72–80
    R 15 – Shuffle Up – Colours ....................................................................... 81–82
    R 16 – Shuffle Up – Numbers ..................................................................... 83–85
    R 17 – Shuffle Up – Days of the Week ....................................................... 86–87
    R 18 – Shuffle Up – Months of the Year ..................................................... 88–90
    R 19 – Which Am I? .................................................................................... 91–93

©Jenny Bell, Sue Cave, Jean Haig
and Brilliant Publications Limited

# Contents

**Files on CD-ROM**

Folders containing interactive files with embedded sounds and videos of actions for:
- F 1 – Colours 1: 6 slides
- F 2 – Colours 2: 6 slides
- F 3 – Numbers 0–5: 6 slides
- F 4 – Numbers 6–10: 6 slides
- F 5 – Family: 6 slides
- F 6 – Sounds, Actions and Spellings: 4 slides

Click on the 'index.html' file in each folder. The file will open in your browser – you do not have to be connected to the Internet. You need to have access to the complete folder to run the index.html file.

Whiteboard files: We have included various forms of whiteboard files, so these resources may be used whether you have a SMART board or Promethean system.

There are three files:
- PSP graphemes with sounds
- PSP images and graphemes with sounds
- PSP images with sounds

Don't have SMART Notebook or Promethean Learning? You can download Promethean ActivInspire for FREE and use the Promethean flipchart versions of the files.

**Resources R1–R18** can be printed out from the teacher book file on the CD-ROM.

**Note**

If you would like to use the resources on a device that does not have a CD drive, please email **info@brilliantpublications.co.uk**, telling us when and from whom you purchased your copy. We will then email you a password and instructions for downloading the files from the Internet.

# PREFACE

*Physical Spanish Phonics* is a sound, action and spelling system (SAS) which we have developed and trialled over many years, both in primary and secondary classrooms with young learners of Spanish and in training sessions with class teachers.

The concept of using kinaesthetic and visual prompts to learn the sounds of the written form of a language is not new. What is unique in *Physical Spanish Phonics* is that most of the actions allotted to each sound have been suggested by the learners themselves. Through consultation and practice, these memorable images and actions are the agreed perceptions of the sounds, from learners new to the Spanish language. This is the strength of *Physical Spanish Phonics*.

*For example:*

*Physical Spanish Phonics* is not a pronunciation guide for purists but it is a tried and tested method for getting to grips with Spanish pronunciation. It is suitable as a teaching aid for specialist and non-specialist language teachers, as well as for students of all ages. It is equally suitable as a self-teaching resource for independent language learners.

The representation of sounds through letters in any language should be seen as a code. It is hoped that *Physical Spanish Phonics* will provide the key needed to unlock this code for all learners of the Spanish language.

# Sounds and Accents

A <u>phoneme</u> is the smallest unit of sound in a language.

A <u>grapheme</u> is the letter (or letters) that represent these units of sound in writing.

*Physical Spanish Phonics* identifies 20 sounds in Castilian Spanish which either do not exist, or whose written form is different in English. The most common representations of letter strings for each of these sounds have been given, but they are not exhaustive. The sound allocated to each grapheme, broadly speaking, corresponds to how they are written phonetically in a bilingual dictionary. However, these can be at odds with dialects of native speakers. The consonants, which have the same, or very similar sounds to those in English, are not included, as they require little practice for a reader of English.

**Note:** the pronunciation of the grapheme 'll' (as in *amarillo*) varies between different regions in Spain. We have chosen to use the phoneme /ʝ/, rather than /ʎ/, as this is the way it is pronounced in central Spain, including Madrid. Both variations are acceptable according to the Real Academia Española.

## Accents

Before we look at accents, it is helpful to understand that there are two basic principles underpinning where the stress lies on a Spanish word:

1. Words that end in a **vowel**, **n** or **s**: the stress is on the penultimate syllable of the word
2. Words that end in a **consonant** (excluding **n** and **s**): the stress is on the last syllable of the word

The main use of accents in Spanish is to highlight words whose accentuation breaks one of these rules, for example: (1)*marrón*,(1) *pájaro*, (2)*mármol*, (2)*árbol* In addition, there are a few occasions where accents are used in Spanish for specific purposes.

- Homophones: to differentiate between words that are pronounced and written the same but have different meanings: **si** (if), **sí** (yes)
- Question words: to show an interrogative word when used in a question, indirect question or embedded question: **¿Qué?** (what)
- Demonstrative pronouns: to differentiate them from demonstrative adjectives: **No vamos a coger este tren, vamos a coger ése** .(We're not going to catch this train, we're going to catch that one.)

# Keywords

## Keywords

To introduce the 20 sounds of *Physical Spanish Phonics*, common words have been selected from: 10 colours; 11 numbers; and 8 family members.

**F1 – Colours 1**
rojo
azul
marrón
amarillo
naranja

**F2 – Colours 2**
gris
negro
verde
blanco
morado

**F3 – Numbers 0–5**
cero
uno
dos
tres
cuatro
cinco

**F4 – Numbers 6–10**
seis
siete
ocho
nueve
diez

**F5 – Family**
madre
padre
niña
niño
abuela*
abuelo*
hermana
hermano

\* *Abuela* and *Abuelo* are abnormalities to the Spanish phonic system. Both /b/ and /β/ are acceptable. However, having consulted with native speakers during recording, it was felt it is more common to use the harder sounding /b/ to distinguish more clearly between the /b/ and /w/ sound.

**Note:** *catorce* (see pages 48 and 85) is an anomaly to the Spanish phonics system. The 'r' is not trilled, although it is before a consonant.

# How to Become familiar with the 20 sounds of Physical Spanish Phonics

The CD-ROM resources of *Physical Spanish Phonics* allow the teacher to become familiar with the actions and the accompanying picture clues. They can also be used by independent adult or mature learners to improve their pronunciation.

The CD-ROM contains separate folders for each group of keywords:
F 1 – colours (*rojo, azul, marrón, amarillo, naranja*)
F 2 – colours (*gris, negro, verde, blanco, morado*)
F 3 – numbers 0–5
F 4 – numbers 6–10
F 5 – family (*madre, padre, niña, niño, abuela, abuelo, hermana, hermano*)

You will only be using the 'index.html' file in each folder. Each 'index.html' file comprises the same format. Follow the process described on pages 9–11 for 'F 1 – Colours 1' for all the keywords. Files F 1–F 5 will introduce you to the 20 sounds, actions and spellings of *Physical Spanish Phonics*. File F 6 will allow you to check your progress.

# F 1 – Colours 1

### Slide 1: Practise the sounds and actions together

Displays video clips of the Spanish sounds and actions that occur in each set of keywords.

- Open up Slide 1 of the file entitled 'F 1 – Colours 1' on the CD-ROM.

- On the slide you will see 9 images, each representing one of the sounds you will encounter from one or more of the five Spanish colour words you are about to learn.

- Click on an image to view a video clip of the sound being produced along with the accompanying action.

- Watch the action; this will help you remember it. Resource R2 (pages 27–31) gives a description of each action.

"Put one hand on your chest patting gently as if you are trying to clear phlegm."

- Practise making the sounds with the accompanying actions.

### Slide 2: Check your knowledge of the sounds

Displays the action images which can be clicked on to hear the individual sound being made by native Spanish speakers.

- Use Slide 2 to practise associating the image with the sound only. Click on an image to hear the sound being pronounced by a native speaker. Then see if you can produce the sound, before clicking on it to check.

## Slide 3: Sound out the phonemes in sequence and pronounce the whole word

Introduces the sequence of sounds for the whole words.

- When you click on a colour, you will be able to see a video clip of a Spanish actor breaking down the whole word into its constituent phonemes. Whenever one of the sounds from Slide 1 occurs, the actor will perform the appropriate action. Practise the sounds, actions and whole words along with the Spanish native speaker.

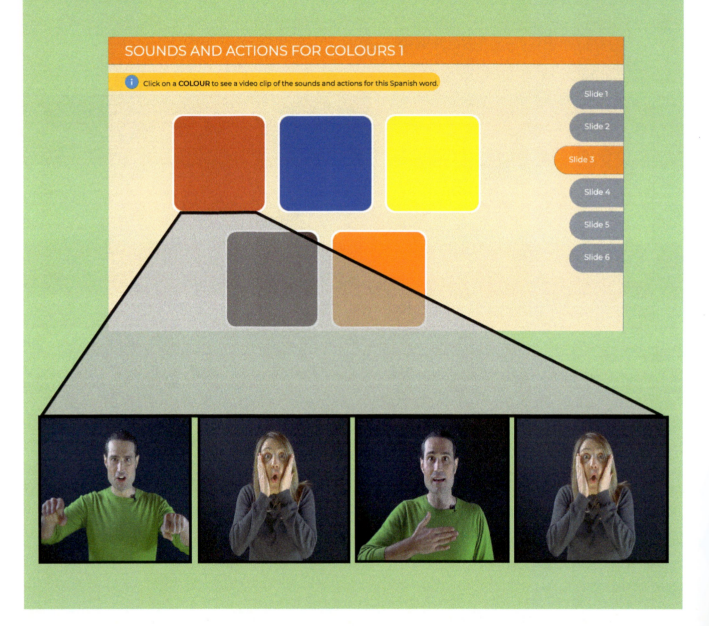

### Slide 4: Associate the letters with each sound

- On Slide 4, you will see the grapheme(s) for each sound to the right of each image. Say the sound and perform the action before clicking on the image to check your pronunciation. Finally, start trying to link the graphemes to the sounds and actions by making a set of two-sided cards from Resources R11 and R12 (pages 57–66) and testing yourself.

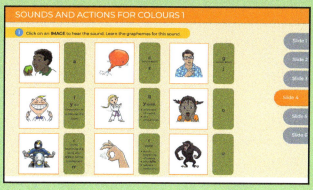

- Being able to hear a sound and associate it with all its graphemes will take time. Don't forget you can always use Resource R1 (page 26) for support.

### Slide 5: Predict the spelling

- Look at Slide 5. Now try to predict the spelling of the word by sounding out the phonemes before clicking on the 'box' to reveal the spelling and hear it as a whole. Clicking on images will enable you to hear individual sounds.

### Slide 6: Practise spelling the word using accompanying actions

- Check your spelling using Slide 6. Use this slide to hear the sounds, watch the actions and reveal the correct spelling of the word.

Repeat the steps for the other keywords:
- F 2 – Colours 2
- F 3 – Numbers 0–5
- F 4 – Numbers 6–10
- F 5 – Family

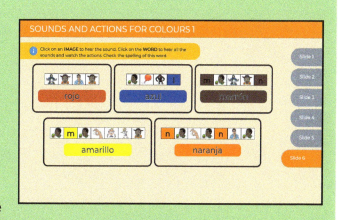

Note: On slides 5 and 6 in F 5 – Family, the 'h' in 'hermano' and 'hermana' is greyed out to show that it is silent.

# F 6. Check your Progress

Once you have met all the sounds, use F 6 – Sounds, Actions and Spellings on the CD-ROM to check your progress.

## Slide 1

- You can watch the video clips for all the sounds and actions.

## Slide 2

- Try saying the sound for each image on the slide before clicking to check.

©Jenny Bell, Sue Cave, Jean Haig and Brilliant Publications Limited

## Slide 3

- By looking in a mirror, you can check your mouth positions with that of a native speaker. Resource R4 (page 33) indicates the mouth position for each symbol.

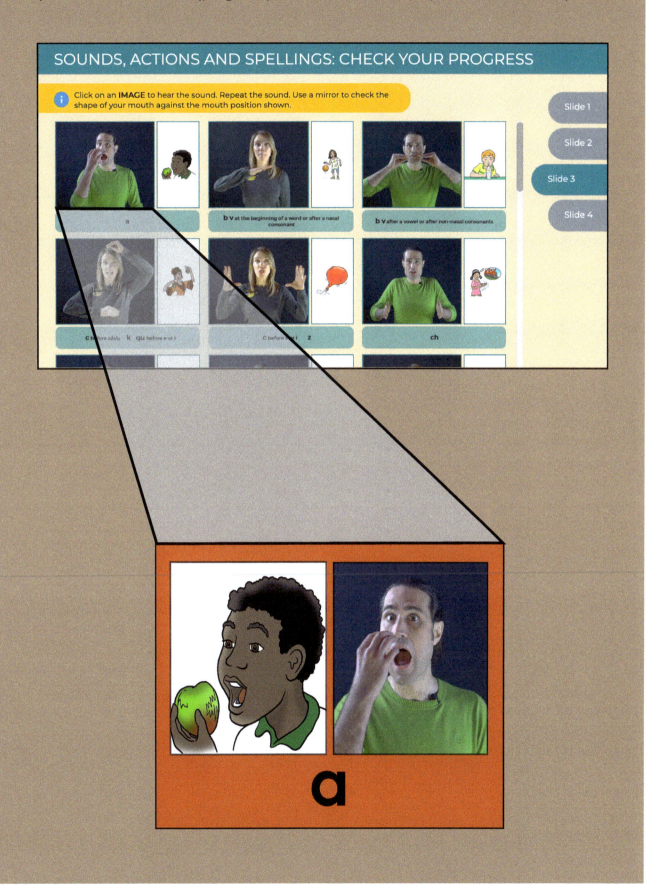

## Slide 4

- If you are using a dictionary to check the pronunciation of a word, you may find it useful to use this slide on the CD-ROM, which shows the International Phonetic Symbol with the accompanying action image.

# The Seven Step Process for Embedding Phonics in Foreign Language Teaching

This is a step by step guide to ensure that a knowledge of phonics is at the heart of teaching a foreign language.

A knowledge of phonics is a shortcut to learning how to recognize and decode language. Learning a new word in a language is not just about knowing its meaning and how it can be used within the context of a sentence, it is also about recognizing the sounds within the word, so it can be understood when heard and read, as well as being reproduced by the speaker in both oral and written form. Expecting students to learn both the sounds and the meaning of a word at the same time is very challenging. The process below separates these two tasks and begins with the sounds of the word, as practice regarding meaning cannot take place until these are firmly embedded.

### Step 1 – Individual sounds
Identify and model, in isolation, the sounds within the word which either do not exist in the student's first language or have different graphemes. Use the accompanying physical action which relates to the sound. Then practise them.

### Step 2 – Blending the sounds in the word
Model the whole word emphasizing each phoneme with an accompanying physical action which relates to the sound. Then practise them.

### Step 3 – Meaning of the word and its sounds
Practise the meaning by relating it to the sounds of the word.

### Step 4 – Graphemes for individual sounds
Present the corresponding grapheme for each sound in the word and practise recognition of it.

### Step 5 – Written form of the whole word
Predict, then reveal the written form of the whole word, highlighting the letters which relate to each new phoneme. Then practise reading, saying and writing the words with physical actions for support.

### Step 6 – Whole word recognition and its sound
Use activities to practise identifying, reading aloud and writing the new word in relation to its meaning.

### Step 7 – Putting words together
Practise putting new words together with others in a sentence.

# CLASSROOM ACTIVITIES FOR PRACTISING PHONICS IN SPANISH LANGUAGE LESSONS

## Preparation

Before starting to teach Spanish, select some words which exist in both Spanish and English but sound quite different and may have different meanings.
For example:

'hospital', 'media', 'idea', 'central', 'once', 'pie' and 'cable'.

Use these as examples for the following preparatory exercises.

- **Lip training**
  To be able to produce each Spanish sound accurately, it is important to have the correct mouth shape. Spanish lips have to work quite hard! Firstly, ask the learners to watch your lips as you mouth each word in both languages and see if they can tell which language you are using.

- **Ear training**
  Before the pupils can begin to imitate Spanish words, it is vital that they are able to distinguish the individual sounds (phonemes) contained within each one. Explain the terms 'phoneme' and 'grapheme' (see page 6), so that you can use them as short cuts in future explanations. Don't forget to check the meaning of these terms regularly. Test out their Spanish ears as they close their eyes and listen to the two pronunciations of the words. Can they put their thumbs up when they hear the Spanish version?

- **Eye training**
  In order to be able to decode text in a different language, learners first have to accept that single letters and combinations of letters (graphemes), with which they are familiar in their own native tongue, can be pronounced or 'decoded' in different ways in other languages.

  Explain that if they gradually learn the single letters and letter combinations that sound different from English, then they will be able to read aloud anything they choose and will be understood, with a high degree of accuracy.

- **Voice training**

    Accurate Spanish sounds can be produced by knowing where to place the tongue and whether to pronounce a sound through the nose, or by using the back of the throat. These positions should be demonstrated and described when introducing unfamiliar sounds.

It is important to point out that it takes a long time to become a proficient reader and speaker of Spanish, but that the effort is worthwhile.

# Classroom Activities for the Seven Step Process

Before embarking on using the following activities, it is essential that you are familiar with the 20 phonic sounds and the accompanying actions. See Resource R1 (page 26) and the instructions on pages 9–14 on how to familiarize yourself with the sounds and actions while using the CD-ROM resources.

Use activities in the following steps 1–6 for each set of keywords in order to introduce the 20 phonic sounds. You will find, that as the students' bank of sound, actions and spelling connections increases, they will not require as much time to learn each set of words. On the other hand they should not be rushed. Through exposure to these words early on in their Spanish language learning, students will encounter all the sounds in *Physical Spanish Phonics*, and will be able to use them as a point of reference for new vocabulary.

## Step 1 – Activities to practise individual sounds

- **Model the actions.** Model the action for each sound and image. For teachers lacking in confidence, use Slide 1 of the appropriate file on the CD-ROM for the keywords to be taught. Click on each image to see a video clip of the sound being produced and the action that will help the pupils to remember it. Otherwise start with Slide 2. Click on the images to hear the sounds being made by the native speakers. Practise saying the sounds and doing the actions, as a group.

- **Actions and sounds.** Ask the class, as a whole group, to do the actions as you call out the different sounds. Then you perform the actions and they produce the corresponding sounds. Invite volunteers to compare their pronunciation with that of a Spanish native speaker by clicking on the images to hear the embedded sound.

- **First to point.** Invite two volunteers to come out and stand in front of the class. Show Slide 1 (on which there are images only) of the appropriate file for each set of keywords. Call out a sound and the first student to point to the correct image, wins a point.

- **First to show.** Distribute the small sets of cards made from Resource R12 (pages 62–66), and identify the ones needed for the particular set of sounds being practised. Call out a sound and award a point to the first student to show the correct image.

- **Pause and say.** Call out two sounds and ask pupils to repeat them. Call out three and repeat the process. Build up to five or six sounds at a time. Then tell them that you will call out a sequence but they should not repeat it aloud until you lower your hand while encouraging them to repeat the sequence in their heads. When you lower your hand, they should try to reproduce the whole sequence.

- **Pick a consonant.** Place a selection of the following consonants in a bag: ch, f, h, j, l, ll, m, n, ñ, p, s, t, v, x, y, z. (Note: avoid using b, d and r as their sound may change, depending on where they appear in a word.) Agree on a vowel sound you want to practise, such as 'e' or 'o'. As each consonant is pulled out of the bag, students say it in front of the vowel sound. This will underline the fact that the phoneme will produce the same sound regardless of what precedes it.

- **Which sound?** As they build up their bank of sound, action and spelling connections, students might find certain phonemes more difficult to identify than others. Discrimination activities are a good idea. For example, to discriminate between the basketball b/v sound and the bottle blowing b/v sound, point out that for the bottle blowing b/v sound, their lips will need to make much less contact. To practise the difference between the drumming d sound and the vibrating phone d sound, they will need to change the position of their tongue from behind their teeth for the drumming d sound, to in between their teeth for the vibrating phone d sound. When they have practised these sounds several times, tell them you are going to call out one of the sounds and they have to do the appropriate action. When they are confident, ask them to shut their eyes as you call out the sounds, to make sure they are not simply copying the actions from those around them.

## Step 2 – Activities to practise blending the sounds in the words

- **Blending the sounds.** Using Slide 3 of the appropriate file, sound out the individual phonemes for each word with the accompanying actions, then blend together to say the whole word. Use the images on the slide to link to the meaning of the word. Alternatively, click on a picture to see a video clip of the whole word being sounded out along with the actions. Practise it altogether.

## Step 3 – Practise the sound and meaning of the words

- **Charades.** Tell them you are going to do the actions for the phonemes in a particular word in the order in which they appear in the word. (Explain that the letters that are sounded the same in English and Spanish are missed out.) They have to guess which one it is. The person who points to the correct image on Slide 3 acts out the next word.

©Jenny Bell, Sue Cave, Jean Haig and Brilliant Publications Limited

- **Throw the beanbag.** When practising colours and numbers, you can give out soft objects that only have one colour (coloured beanbags are ideal) or foam numbers. Call out a phoneme students have learnt and if they think the colour of the object or the number they are holding contains that sound, invite them to throw their object into the centre of the room. The students can then discuss whether the choices were appropriate.

- **Splat the word with the phoneme.** Invite two volunteers to come out and stand in front of Slide 3 of the appropriate file for each set of keywords. Call out a sound and the first learner to point to any image containing that phoneme, wins a point.

- **Sounds in a story.** Read out a simple story in which there are plenty of examples of the sounds being practised and ask students to do the appropriate action each time they hear a particular phoneme. If they are able to follow the text at the same time, they might begin to notice which letters produce that sound. This will prepare them for the next stage in the process.

The sounds, together with the meaning of the new words, should now be practised using a variety of activities for developing oracy skills. Any mispronunciation can be corrected by using the sound, action and spelling system.

## Step 4 – Activities for recognizing the graphemes

- **Write in the air.** Once you are confident that students are producing the sounds correctly, reveal the corresponding highlighted graphemes on Slide 4 of the appropriate file. As students say the sounds, invite them to practise writing them in the air, on their hands or on mini-whiteboards. This simple kinaesthetic activity helps many students to internalize the sound/spelling connections.

- **Write the grapheme.** Call out a phoneme and ask the students to copy the correct grapheme from Slide 4 onto a mini-whiteboard. Ask them to discuss what they have chosen with a partner before asking someone for the answer.

- **Listen and show.** Make back-to-back sets of Resources R11 and R12 (pages 57–66) (taking care you match the correct image and grapheme). Identify the cards that are needed for the set of keywords being practised and put the rest to one side. The side with the image and the accompanying grapheme should be uppermost.

   Students might like to work in pairs initially. Call out a phoneme and see if each pair can produce the correct card. Repeat with the grapheme only side uppermost.

- **First to show.** Call out a phoneme and the first to produce the appropriate card, wins a point.

- **Turn and read.** Using the cards already made from Resources R11 and R12 (pages 57–66), place them in an agreed order on each table, image and grapheme side

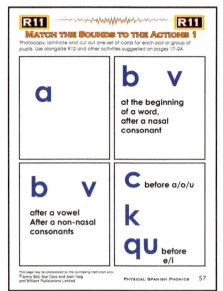

facing upwards. Have each group read along the line of cards. Ask them to turn over one specific card and read the line out again. Ask them to turn over a second and now read the line out. Continue turning over the cards until they are reading just the graphemes. Alter the order of the cards to see if they can still read them. To make sure each individual's knowledge is secure, invite them to work in pairs, turning the pictures back into view when necessary.

- **Fire and hire.** Show a card with a grapheme on it. Invite the students to identify the sound (using a supporting action if necessary). The person who can produce the sound correctly now takes ownership of the card at the front of the class. Distribute more cards. Tell those at the front that every time they hear you use 'their' sound they have one second to lift it above their heads. If they fail to do it on time, they are 'fired' and they have to 'hire' someone else. The children who are watching are usually keen to have their turn and try hard to learn the sound/spelling connections so that they don't get fired when it is their turn.

- **Splat the grapheme.** Write a selection of graphemes on the board or display Resource R11 cards (pages 57–61). Two students compete to be the first to touch the correct spellings for the phonemes you call out. *Splat the grapheme* can also be played in teams. The first player in each team comes to the board and the teacher calls out a phoneme. The winner goes to the back of the team and the losing player is eliminated from the game. The game continues until one team runs out of players. As they become more confident, they can play *Splat the grapheme* in pairs with the selection of graphemes copied onto a piece of paper or mini-whiteboard.

- **Sing the phonemes.** Display a selection of graphemes on the board. Choose a well-known tune and invite the learners to sing the phonemes as you point to them, replacing the usual words of the song.

- **Phonic sing-song sequences.** Working in groups, invite pupils to put a selection of cards made from Resource R11 (pages 57–61) grapheme-side-up in whichever order they like and practise singing them to a tune of their choice whilst performing the actions. Some groups might need you to suggest suitable tunes. A performance of all the sequences in front of the whole class at the end of the session is always great fun. Those who don't like singing could produce their own sequences in groups and then perform them as a rap or as a substitute for dialogue in a dramatic scene.

- **Phonic loto (bingo).** Pupils choose an agreed number of graphemes from a selection on the board and write them down on a piece of paper or a mini-whiteboard. As you call out the sounds, they look to see if they are amongst their choices. Pupils circle the ones they think have been called out until one of them has none left on their sheet of paper or mini-whiteboard. This is the point at which the learner calls out 'Loto' and reads out their selection for you to check that they are actually the winner.

- **Phonic Blockbusters.** Make a Blockbuster style grid and fill it with graphemes. Display it on the board. Students are invited to choose a starting point on one side of the grid and read out graphemes until they reach the other side of the grid. If they reach a grapheme they don't know, they can move sideways until they find one they know and then move forward from there. If plenty of students are finding it easy, use a timer to see who can get through the grid the quickest.

- **Spell the grapheme.** Using Resource R13 (pages 67–71) invite the students to fill in the missing graphemes for each image. By laminating these resources and using water-based marker pens, they can be reused. You can also monitor their progress by challenging the students to write down the graphemes for the phonemes you call out without the support of the images. Reveal the correct spelling.

- **Which Am I?** Choose 5 or 6 phonemes that you wish to practise. Give students the grapheme cards for these phonemes (using Resource R11, pages 57-61). Say a word which uses the phoneme and ask them to hold up the correct card(s). Sample words are given on Resource R19 (pages 91–93). (Please note: depending on the sounds you chose to practise, children may hold up more than one grapheme for each word.)

## Step 5 – Activities for practising the spelling of whole words

- **Predict a spelling.** With the help of the actions and the small card sets (Resource R11 pages 57–61), ask students to predict the spellings of the whole words being practised. Show them Slide 5 of the appropriate file and, using the images and letters on the slides as prompts, ask the children to predict the spelling of the word on mini-whiteboards. Click on a 'box' to reveal the spelling. Children can check it against their prediction.

  The children will notice that the '**h**' appears in outline only in the words 'hermano' and 'hermana'. This is because it is a silent letter. If this is the first time they have encountered the silent letter '**h**' in Spanish words, discuss whether they know of any silent letters in other languages.

  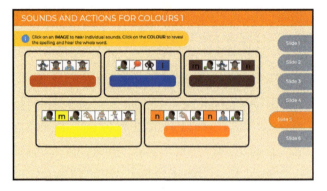

  Laminate copies of Resource 1 (page 26) so that it can be used with water-based marker pens and wiped clean afterwards. Distribute them among your students. To challenge students further, call out an unfamiliar word and ask them to circle/copy down all the graphemes they can detect. See how close they can get to predicting the actual spelling.

- **Colour Match.** Colour Match cards (R14, page 72–80), laminate and photocopy both the spell card and the grapheme cards. (Cut out and shuffle the grapheme cards only.) Give a set of colours to pupils to match up.

  *Tip: Once laminated, use velcro sticky fasteners on the cards so the pupils can attach them together.*

  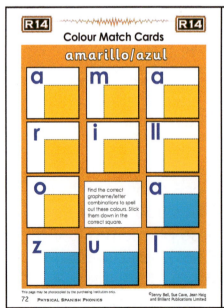
  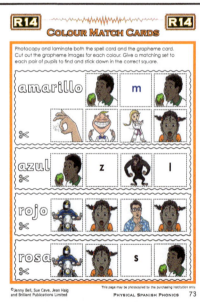

22  PHYSICAL SPANISH PHONICS

©Jenny Bell, Sue Cave, Jean Haig and Brilliant Publications Limited

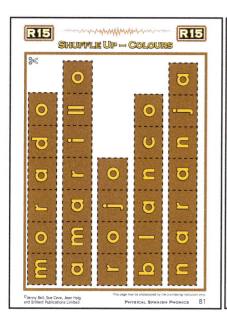 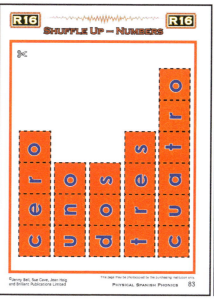 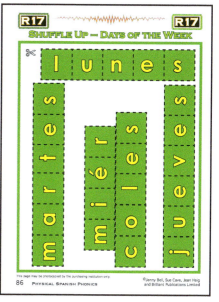

- **Word stations.** Make copies of the appropriate Resources R15–18 (pages 81–90) and cut these pages into the marked squares. Put the constituent letters/phonemes for each word into a separate envelope and label the envelopes Station 1, Station 2, etc. Place the envelopes around the room with as few obstacles as possible around them so that the groups can access them easily. Each group of students has a piece of paper on which to write down the answers. Play some music and invite the students to walk from station to station. When the music stops, the group empties the contents of the envelope on to a table and tries to reconstruct the word. The designated scribe for each group writes down the word on an answer sheet with the headings: Station 1, Station 2, etc. After all the stations have been visited, check the answer sheets and award points for each correct answer. Celebrate the results!

- **Table card game.** Depending on the words being practised, make appropriate sets from Resources R15–R18 (pages 81–90). Give a set to each group of four learners. Deal the cards equally. The first person to play will be the one with the first phoneme of the first word in the series. (Colours could be displayed in a particular order on the board.) The person to their right looks to see whether he/she has the next sound in the word. If he/she doesn't, they knock on the table and the turn passes to the person on their right. The winner is the person who has no cards left.

- **Find your group.** Using a set of the same resources as for the Table card game, give each student one card. Invite the whole group to move around the room and ask whoever they meet what sound they have on their card. If the sounds can be added together to form part of one of the keywords, they join forces to find other students to complete their word.

- **Phonic Happy Families.** Distribute a set of cards made from Resources R15–R18 (or a selection of them from pages 81–90) amongst a group of pupils. Each learner examines the cards in their 'hand'. When it is their turn, pupils will try to make up whole words by asking individual members of the group for particular graphemes to add to the ones in front of them. If the person asked has the grapheme requested, it is handed over. If not, their turn is over and play passes to the next player. The winner is the person who has the largest number of completed words and no cards left.

- **Phonic hangman.** This is similar to normal hangman except that instead of using one dash to represent each single letter, you write a short dash for a one-letter sound and a long dash for a sound made up of two letters. Those guessing have to produce the whole grapheme before you convert the dashes to letters.

### Step 6 – Practise the spelling and meaning of the whole word

- **Practise spelling and meaning.** Practise reading aloud and writing the new words using a variety of activities for developing literacy skills to practise meaning.

# Create Your Own Resources

Once you have presented all the keywords, thereby introducing each of the 20 phonemes, your students will continue to need support when encountering new words. Resources 9 and 10 (pages 52–56) spell out the Days of the Week and Months of the Year using **PSP** images. Each time you introduce a new set of words follow the seven-step process. You can copy and paste the images with embedded sound files in the Smart Board gallery files or Promethean flipchart files to create your own resources, like those provided for the keywords. On the CD-ROM you will find SMART board gallery files and Promethean flipchart files for:

- PSP graphemes with sounds
- PSP images and graphemes with sounds
- PSP images with sounds

All the whiteboard files can be edited.

As your students become more familiar with the sound and letter connections, you can omit Step 1 of the process and introduce new vocabulary by modelling the whole word with sound, action and spelling support and then move on more quickly to the graphemes and written form of the word to practise the meaning. Eventually, once your students have a very good grasp of the sound of graphemes in a word, new language can be introduced by presenting its written form and by asking your students to sound it out. This is the ultimate goal.

©Jenny Bell, Sue Cave, Jean Haig and Brilliant Publications Limited

# Further Practice and Support

- **Sound, Action and Spelling system wall displays.** As each phoneme is introduced, display the relevant image from the phonics frieze (Resource R5, pages 34–43) until all are available for easy reference on the classroom wall.

- **Working wall.** Set aside a working wall for new vocabulary divided into sections, one for each phoneme you wish to highlight. As new words are encountered, add them to the appropriate section.

- **Phonics for labelling.** Instead of numbering or writing A, B, C, etc, on the back of flashcards used for playing games, try labelling them with graphemes instead as there is a constant need for review, reinforcement and practice.

- **Sound, Action and Spelling mat.** Print the Sound, Action, Spelling Chart (Resource R1, page 26). Either laminate to create a 'mat' and distribute as a classroom resource or provide a copy for each student to stick into their workbook. Use this mat or sheet as a handy reference for decoding new words as they are encountered.

The teacher book is available as a PDF on the CD-ROM, enabling resources R1– R18 on pages 26–90 to be printed easily.

# SOUNDS, ACTIONS AND SPELLINGS

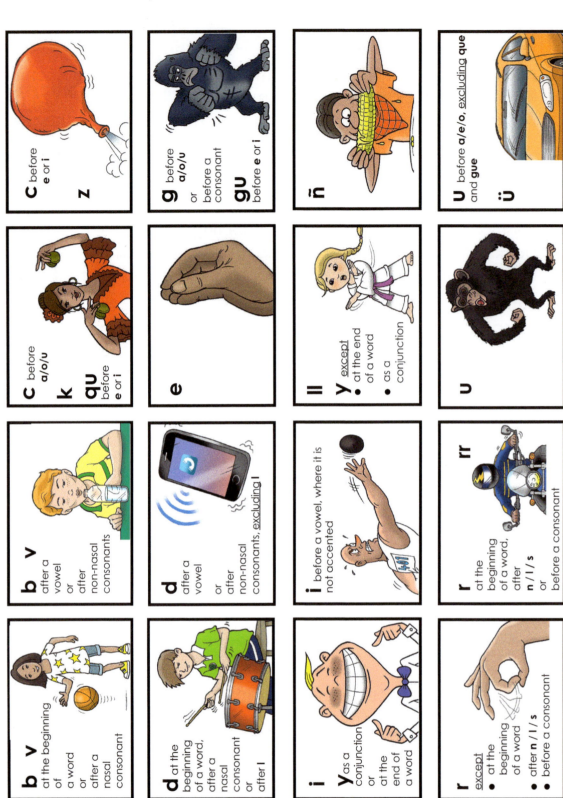

26 PHYSICAL SPANISH PHONICS

©Jenny Bell, Sue Cave, Jean Haig and Brilliant Publications Limited

This page may be photocopied by the purchasing institution only.

# DESCRIPTION OF PHYSICAL ACTIONS

Open your mouth wide as though you are about to take a bite from an apple.

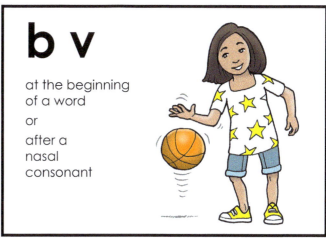

Bounce a large ball on the ground, imitate the noise made when patting the ball.

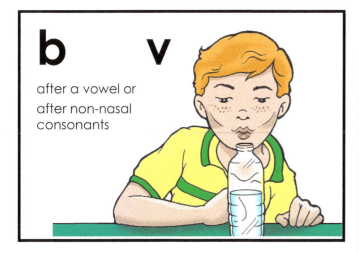

Hold the bottle up to your mouth and gently blow across the top of it. Purse your lips and gently blow out.

You are a Spanish dancer playing the castanets.

# DESCRIPTION OF PHYSICAL ACTIONS

**c** before **e** or **i**

**z**

You are holding a blown up balloon between your fingers. Slowly release the pressure and allow the air to escape.

**ch**

Move your arms in a forward and backward rolling motion pretending to be a train.

**d** at the beginning of a word, after a nasal consonant or after **l**

You are a drummer playing the drums.

**d** after a vowel or after non-nasal consonants, <u>excluding</u> **l**

Hand held out-stretched, palm upward. Shake hand vigorously from side-to-side as if it is vibrating.

This page may be photocopied by the purchasing institution only.

28   PHYSICAL SPANISH PHONICS

©Jenny Bell, Sue Cave, Jean Haig and Brilliant Publications Limited

# DESCRIPTION OF PHYSICAL ACTIONS

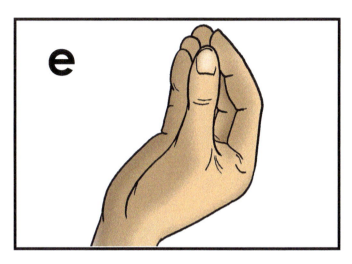

Fingers and thumb pointing upwards, making an exasperated sigh.

You are a gorilla beating your chest with two fists.

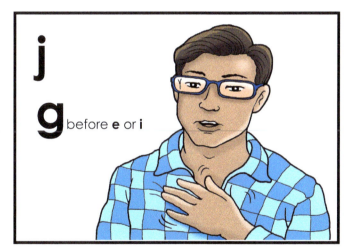

Put one hand on your chest, patting gently as if trying to clear phlegm.

Show all your teeth in a cheesy grin.

©Jenny Bell, Sue Cave, Jean Haig and Brilliant Publications Limited

This page may be photocopied by the purchasing institution only.

**PHYSICAL SPANISH PHONICS**

# Description of Physical Actions

**i** before a vowel, where it is not accented

You are a shot-putter really exerting yourself in a throw. The effort can be seen on your face.

**ll**
**y** except
- at the end of a word
- as a conjunction

You are just about to exert a throw on your opponent.

**ñ**

You are gnawing noisily on a corn-on-the-cob.

**o**

You have just had a big shock.

# DESCRIPTION OF PHYSICAL ACTIONS

**r**

except
- at the beginning of a word,
- after **n / l / s**

or
- before a consonant

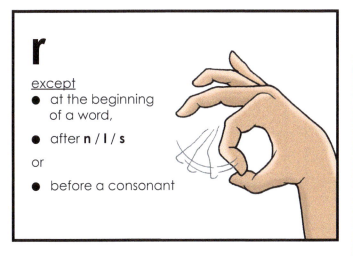

Hand held up in an "ok" position and then flick your finger out against your thumb.

**r**  **rr**

at the beginning of a word,
after **n / l / s**
or
before a consonant

Riding along on your motorbike, you are showing off so you start revving it up.

**U**

Pretend to be a chimpanzee! Bring your hands up bent towards your armpits, bend your knees and bounce.

**U**

**Ü** before **a/e/o**, excluding **que** and **gue**

Arms moving side-to-side in a windscreen-wiper motion.

©Jenny Bell, Sue Cave, Jean Haig and Brilliant Publications Limited

# International Phonetic Symbols with Images and Actions

R3

| | | | |
|---|---|---|---|
| /a/ | /b/ | /β/ | /k/ |
| /tʃ/ | /d/ | /ð/ | /e/ |
| /x/ | /i/ | /j/ | /ɲ/ |
| /o/ | /ɾ/ | /r/ | /u/ |
| | | /θ/ | |
| | | /g/ | |
| | | /ʃ/ | |
| | | /w/ | |

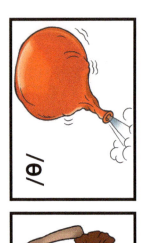

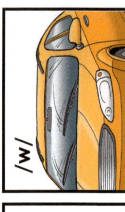

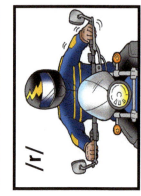

©Jenny Bell, Sue Cave, Jean Haig and Brilliant Publications Limited

# International Phonetic Symbols
## With Mouth Positions

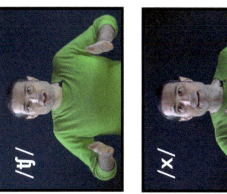

# R5 Sounds, actions and spellings

**b v** at the beginning of a word or after a nasal consonant

*Examples:* **b**lanco, **v**erde
ha**m**burguesa, i**n**vento

**a**

*Example:* **b**la**n**co

34 Physical Spanish Phonics

©Jenny Bell, Sue Cave, Jean Haig and Brilliant Publications Limited

# Sounds, Actions and Spellings

**R5**

**c** before a/o/u  **k**  **qu** before e or i

**Examples:** <u>c</u>apital, <u>c</u>ultura, <u>c</u>ocodrilo, <u>k</u>ilo, <u>qu</u>é, mos<u>qu</u>ito

**b**  **v** after a vowel or after non-nasal consonants

**Examples:** de<u>b</u>ate, nue<u>v</u>e, ál<u>b</u>um, reser<u>v</u>ar

©Jenny Bell, Sue Cave, Jean Haig and Brilliant Publications Limited

This page may be photocopied by the purchasing institution only.

Physical Spanish Phonics   35

# Sounds, Actions and Spellings

**R5**

**ch**

*Example:* **o<u>ch</u>o**

**z**

**c** before e or i

*Examples:* **<u>c</u>ero, <u>c</u>inco, a<u>z</u>ul**

36 Physical Spanish Phonics

©Jenny Bell, Sue Cave, Jean Haig and Brilliant Publications Limited

This page may be photocopied by the purchasing institution only.

# R5 Sounds, actions and spellings

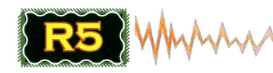

**d** after a vowel, after non-nasal consonants, excluding l

*Examples:* **me‍dia, sar‍dina, ver‍de**

**d** at the beginning of a word, after a nasal consonant or after l

*Examples:* **dónde, indicar, falda**

©Jenny Bell, Sue Cave, Jean Haig and Brilliant Publications Limited

PHYSICAL SPANISH PHONICS

# R5 Sounds, actions and spellings

**g** before a/o/u or before a consonant  **gu** before e or i

Examples: <u>g</u>ala, man<u>g</u>o, sin<u>g</u>ular, ne<u>g</u>ro, hambur<u>gu</u>esa, <u>gu</u>itarra,

**e**

Examples: tr<u>e</u>s, di<u>e</u>z

38 Physical Spanish Phonics

©Jenny Bell, Sue Cave, Jean Haig and Brilliant Publications Limited

# Sounds, actions and spellings

## R5

### y — as a conjunction or at the end of a word

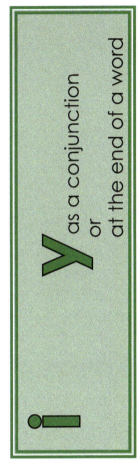

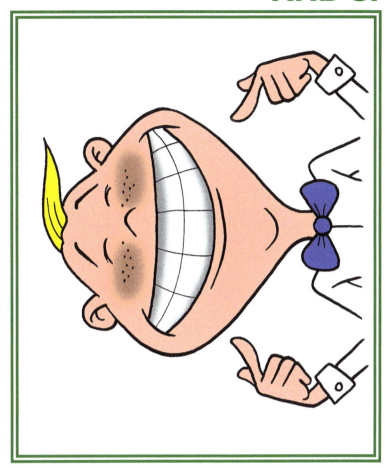

**Examples:** gris, y (and), hay, rey

### g — before e or i
### j

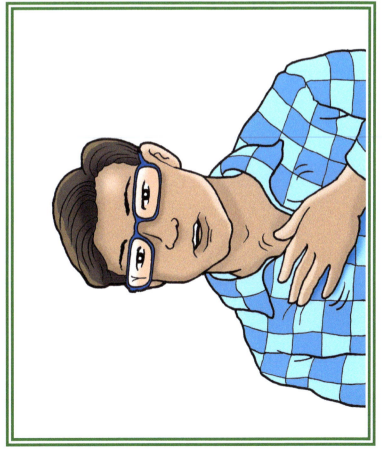

**Examples:** rojo, agenda, gimnasio

©Jenny Bell, Sue Cave, Jean Haig and Brilliant Publications Limited

This page may be photocopied by the purchasing institution only.

# R5 Sounds, actions and spellings

**y** except
- at the end of a word
- as a conjunction

= ll

Examples: **amari_ll_o, pla_y_a**

**i** before a vowel, where it is not accented

Example: **s_i_ete**

40 PHYSICAL SPANISH PHONICS

©Jenny Bell, Sue Cave, Jean Haig and Brilliant Publications Limited

This page may be photocopied by the purchasing institution only.

# R5 Sounds, actions and spellings

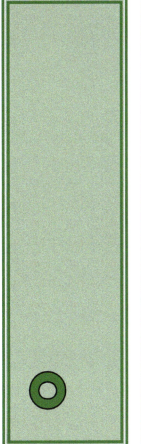

o

*Examples:* **blanco, rojo**

n

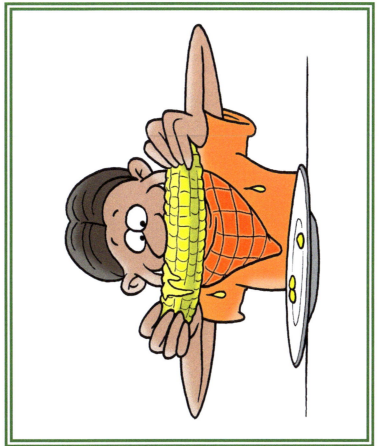

*Examples:* **niño, araña**

Physical Spanish Phonics   41

# R5 Sounds, actions and spellings

**rr**

r at the beginning of a word, after n / l / s or before a consonant

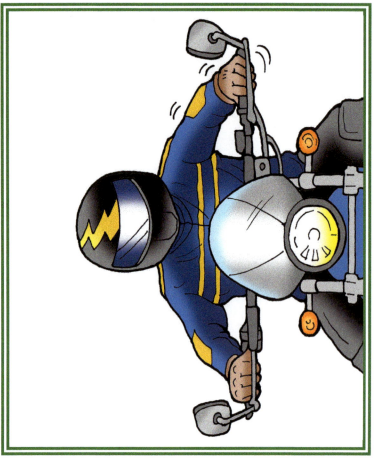

**Examples: r**osa, En**r**ique, al**r**ededor, Is**r**ael, ma**rr**ón, ve**r**de

**r** except
- at the beginning of a word
- after n / l / s
- before a consonant

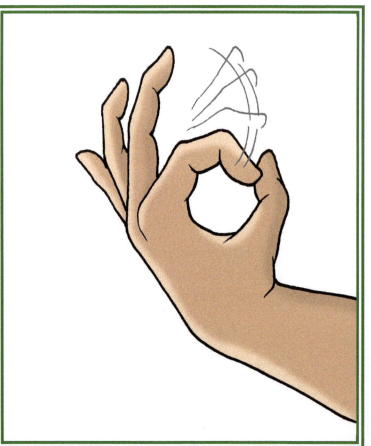

**Examples:** mo**r**ado, pad**r**e

42 Physical Spanish Phonics

©Jenny Bell, Sue Cave, Jean Haig and Brilliant Publications Limited

This page may be photocopied by the purchasing institution only.

# SOUNDS, ACTIONS AND SPELLINGS

**ü**

**U** before a/e/o, excluding **que** and **gue**

*Examples:* **pingüino, cuatro, nueve, antiguo**

**u**

*Example:* **azul**

PHYSICAL SPANISH PHONICS  43

# COLOURS

# Numbers 0–4

0 cero

1 uno

2 dos

3 tres

4 cuatro

# Numbers 5–9

5 cinco

6 seis

7 siete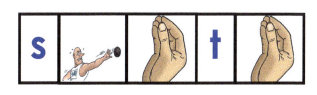

8 ocho

9 nueve

# Numbers 10–14

10
**diez**

11
**once**

12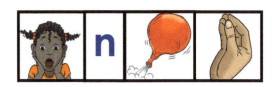
**doce**

13
**trece**

14
**catorce**

# FAMILY

h**ermano**

h**ermana**

**abuelo**

**abuela**

# FAMILY

**niño**

**niña**

**padre**

**madre**

# FAMILY

**primo**

**prima**

**tío**

**tía**

# Days of the Week

**lunes**

**martes**

**miércoles**

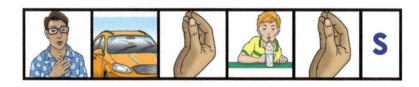

**jueves**

# Days of the Week

**viernes**

**sábado**

**domingo**

# MONTHS OF THE YEAR

**enero**

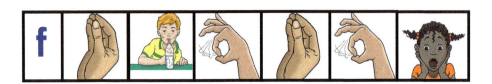

**febrero**

**marzo**

**abril**

# MONTHS OF THE YEAR

**mayo**

**junio**

**julio**

**agosto**

# MONTHS OF THE YEAR

## septiembre

## octubre

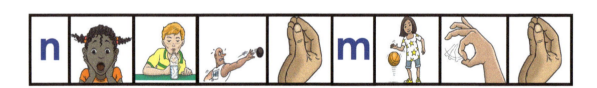

## noviembre

## diciembre

## Match the Sounds to the Actions – Grapheme Only

Photocopy, laminate and cut out one set of cards for each pair or group of pupils. Use alongside R12 and for other activities suggested on pages 17–24.

| | |
|---|---|
| **a** | **b v** at the beginning of a word or after a nasal consonant |
| **b v** after a vowel or after non-nasal consonants | **c** before a/o/u <br> **k** <br> **qu** before **e** or **i** |

This page may be photocopied by the purchasing institution only.
©Jenny Bell, Sue Cave, Jean Haig and Brilliant Publications Limited

PHYSICAL SPANISH PHONICS  57

## Match the Sounds to the Actions – Grapheme Only

Photocopy, laminate and cut out one set of cards for each pair or group of pupils. Use alongside R12 and for other activities suggested on pages 17–24.

| | |
|---|---|
| **c**<br>**before e** or **i**<br><br>**z** | **ch** |
| **d**<br><br>at the beginning of a word, after a nasal consonant or after l | **d**<br><br>after a vowel or after non-nasal consonants, <u>excluding</u> l |

This page may be photocopied by the purchasing institution only.
©Jenny Bell, Sue Cave, Jean Haig and Brilliant Publications Limited

## Match the Sounds to the Actions – Grapheme Only

Photocopy, laminate and cut out one set of cards for each pair or group of pupils. Use alongside R12 and for other activities suggested on pages 17–24.

| | |
|---|---|
| **e** | **g** before a/o/u or before a consonant  **gu** before e or i |
| **j**  **g** before e or i | **i**  **y** as a conjunction or at the end of a word |

## Match the Sounds to the Actions – Grapheme Only

Photocopy, laminate and cut out one set of cards for each pair or group of pupils. Use alongside R12 and for other activities suggested on pages 17–24.

| | |
|---|---|
| **i** before a vowel, where it is not accented | **ll** **y** except<br>• at the end of a word<br>• as a conjunction |
|  | **o** |

60  PHYSICAL SPANISH PHONICS

This page may be photocopied by the purchasing institution only.
©Jenny Bell, Sue Cave, Jean Haig and Brilliant Publications Limited

## Match the Sounds to the Actions – Grapheme Only

Photocopy, laminate and cut out one set of cards for each pair or group of pupils. Use alongside R12 and for other activities suggested on pages 17–24.

| | |
|---|---|
| **r** <u>except</u><br>● at the beginning of a word<br>● after n/l/s<br>● before a consonant | **r    rr**<br>at the beginning of a word, after n/l/s or before a consonant |
| **u** | **ü**<br><br>**u** before a/e/o, <u>excluding</u> que or gue |

## MATCH THE SOUNDS TO THE ACTIONS – IMAGE AND GRAPHEME

Photocopy, laminate and cut out one set of cards for each pair or group of pupils. Use alongside R11 and for other activities suggested on pages 17–24.

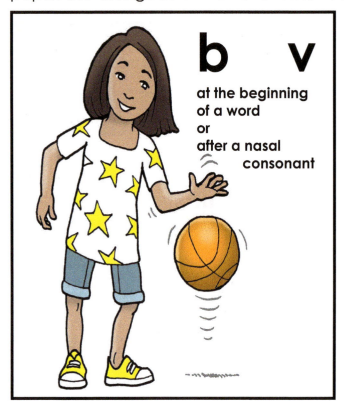

**b v** at the beginning of a word or after a nasal consonant

**a**

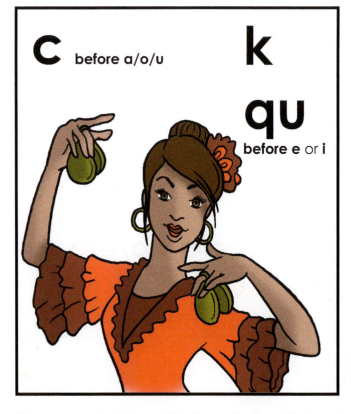

**c** before a/o/u

**k**

**qu** before e or i

**b v** after a vowel or after non-nasal consonants

This page may be photocopied by the purchasing institution only.

©Jenny Bell, Sue Cave, Jean Haig and Brilliant Publications Limited

PHYSICAL SPANISH PHONICS

## MATCH THE SOUNDS TO THE ACTIONS – IMAGE AND GRAPHEME

Photocopy, laminate and cut out one set of cards for each pair or group of pupils. Use alongside R11 and for other activities suggested on pages 17–24.

**ch**

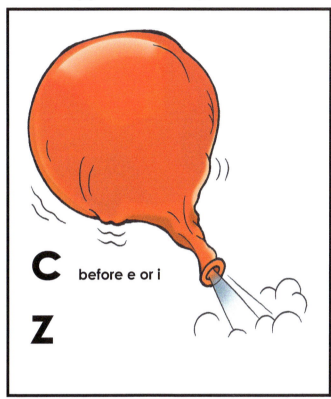

**c** before e or i
**z**

**d** after a vowel
or
after a non-nasal consonant, excluding l

**d** at the beginning of a word,
after a nasal consonant
or
after l

## Match the Sounds to the Actions – Image and Grapheme

Photocopy, laminate and cut out one set of cards for each pair or group of pupils. Use alongside R11 and for other activities suggested on pages 17–24.

**g** before a/o/u or before a consonant

**gu** before e or i

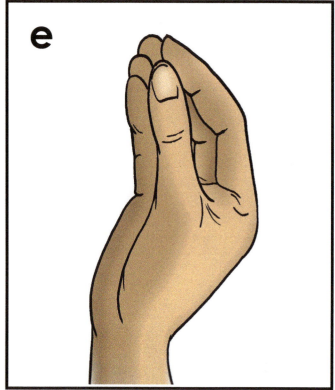

**e**

**i**

**y** as a conjunction or at the end of a word

**j**

**g** before e or i

## Match the Sounds to the Actions – Image and Grapheme

Photocopy, laminate and cut out one set of cards for each pair or group of pupils. Use alongside R11 and for other activities suggested on pages 17–24.

**ll**

**y** except
- at the end of a word
- as a conjunction

**i** before a vowel, where it is not accented

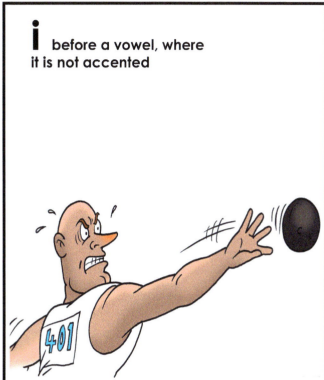

**o**

**ñ**

## Match the Sounds to the Actions – Image and Grapheme

Photocopy, laminate and cut out one set of cards for each pair or group of pupils. Use alongside R11 and for other activities suggested on pages 17–24.

**r** at the beginning of a word,
after n/l/s
or
before a consonant

**rr**

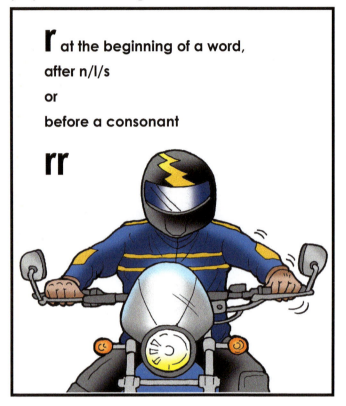

**r** except
- at the beginning of a word
- after n/l/s
- before a consonant

**ü**

**u** before a/e/o, excluding que or gue

**u**

This page may be photocopied by the purchasing institution only.

©Jenny Bell, Sue Cave, Jean Haig and Brilliant Publications Limited

PHYSICAL SPANISH PHONICS

# Spell the Grapheme

Photocopy, laminate and cut out one set of cards for each pair or group of pupils. Ask your students to fill in the blanks with the correct graphemes.

©Jenny Bell, Sue Cave, Jean Haig and Brilliant Publications Limited

This page may be photocopied by the purchasing institution only.

PHYSICAL SPANISH PHONICS 67

# Spell the Grapheme

Photocopy, laminate and cut out one set of cards for each pair or group of pupils. Ask your students to fill in the blanks with the correct grapheme.

## Spell the Grapheme

Photocopy, laminate and cut out one set of cards for each pair or group of pupils. Ask your students to fill in the blanks with the correct grapheme.

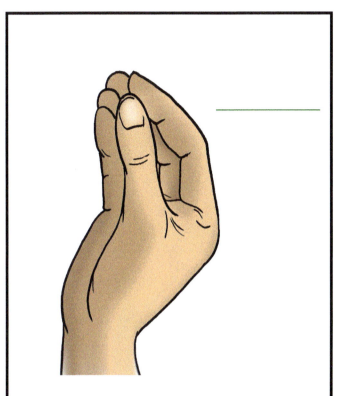

©Jenny Bell, Sue Cave, Jean Haig and Brilliant Publications Limited

This page may be photocopied by the purchasing institution only.

# SPELL THE GRAPHEME

Photocopy, laminate and cut out one set of cards for each pair or group of pupils. Ask your students to fill in the blanks with the correct grapheme.

This page may be photocopied by the purchasing institution only.

70   PHYSICAL SPANISH PHONICS

©Jenny Bell, Sue Cave, Jean Haig and Brilliant Publications Limited

## SPELL THE GRAPHEME

Photocopy, laminate and cut out one set of cards for each pair or group of pupils. Ask your students to fill in the blanks with the correct grapheme.

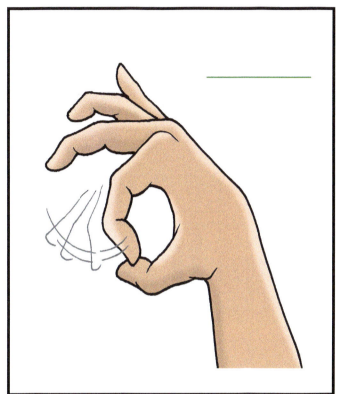
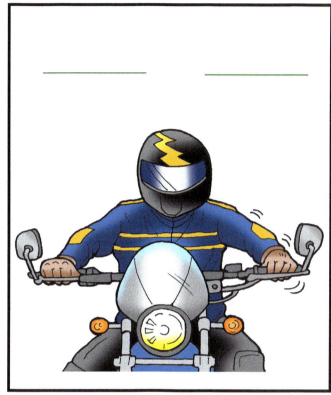

PHYSICAL SPANISH PHONICS

## Colour Match Cards

# amarillo/azul

| a | m | a |
| r | i | ll |
| o | *Find the correct grapheme/letter combinations to spell out these colours. Stick them down in the correct square.* | a |
| z | u | l |

# Colour Match Cards

Photocopy and laminate both the spell card and the grapheme card. Cut out the grapheme images for each colour. Give a matching set to each pair of pupils to find and stick down in the correct square.

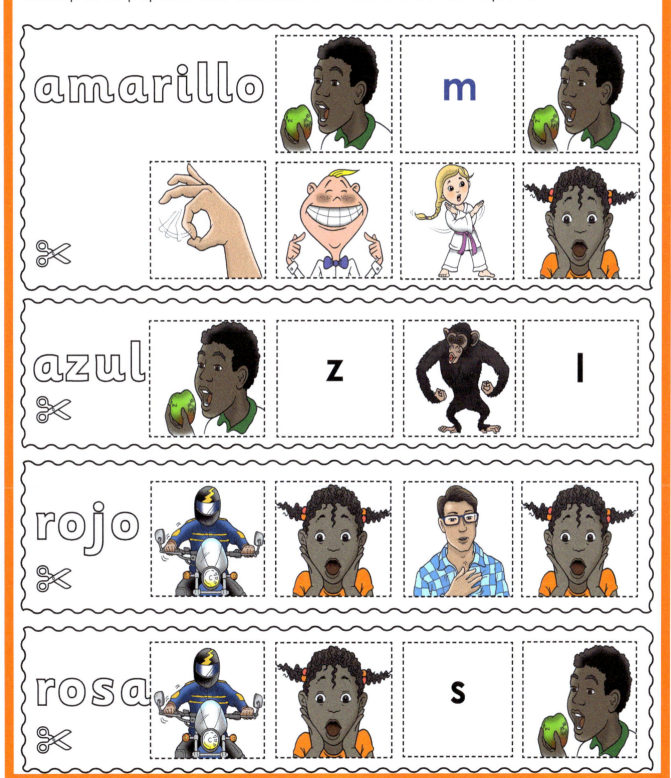

PHYSICAL SPANISH PHONICS

## Colour Match Cards

### rojo/rosa/gris

| r | o | j |
|---|---|---|
| o | r | o |
| s | a | g |
| r | i | s |

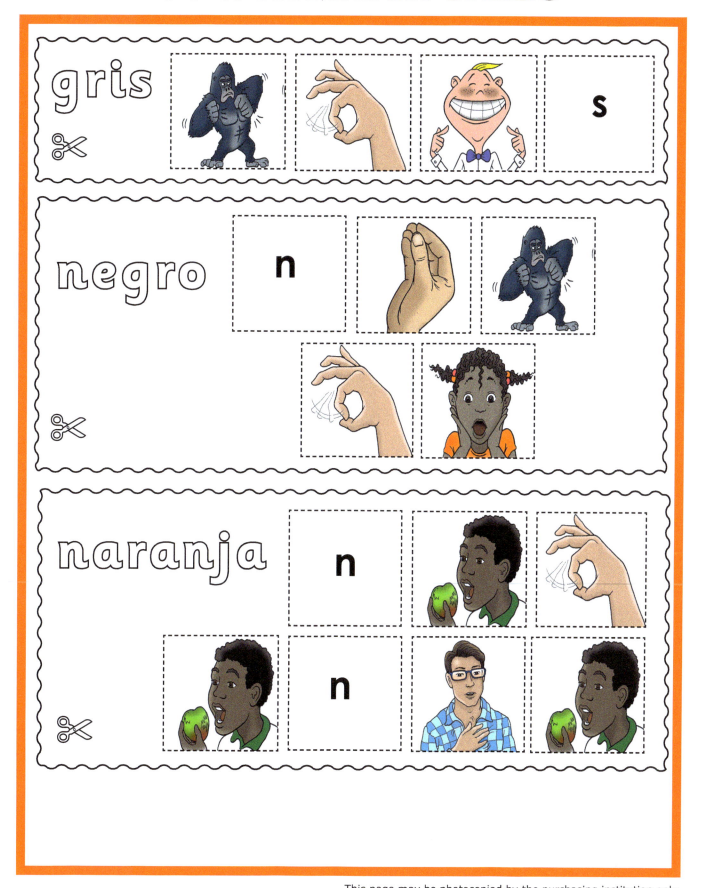

## Colour Match Cards

### negro/naranja

| n | e | g |
|---|---|---|
| r | o | n |
| a | r | a |
| n | j | a |

## Colour Match Cards

# blanco/marrón

| b | l | a |
| n | c | o |
| m | a | rr |
| | ó | n |

## Colour Match Cards

## Colour Match Cards

# verde/morado

| v | e | r |
|---|---|---|
| d | e |   |

| m | o | r |
|---|---|---|
| a | d | o |

## Colour Match Cards

### verde

 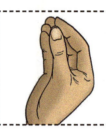 

### morado

m

# Shuffle Up – Colours

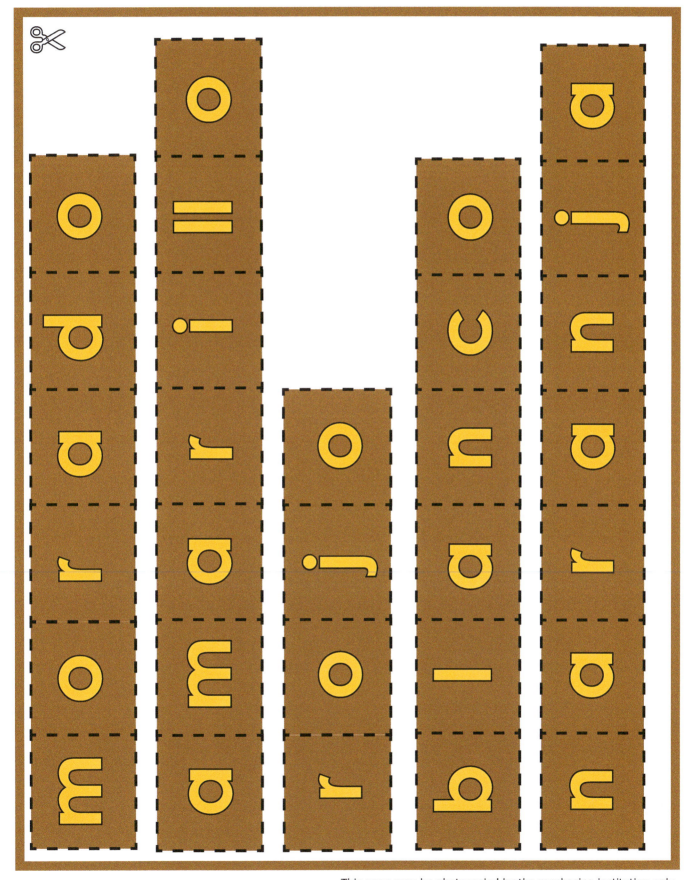

## Shuffle Up – Colours

# Shuffle Up – Numbers

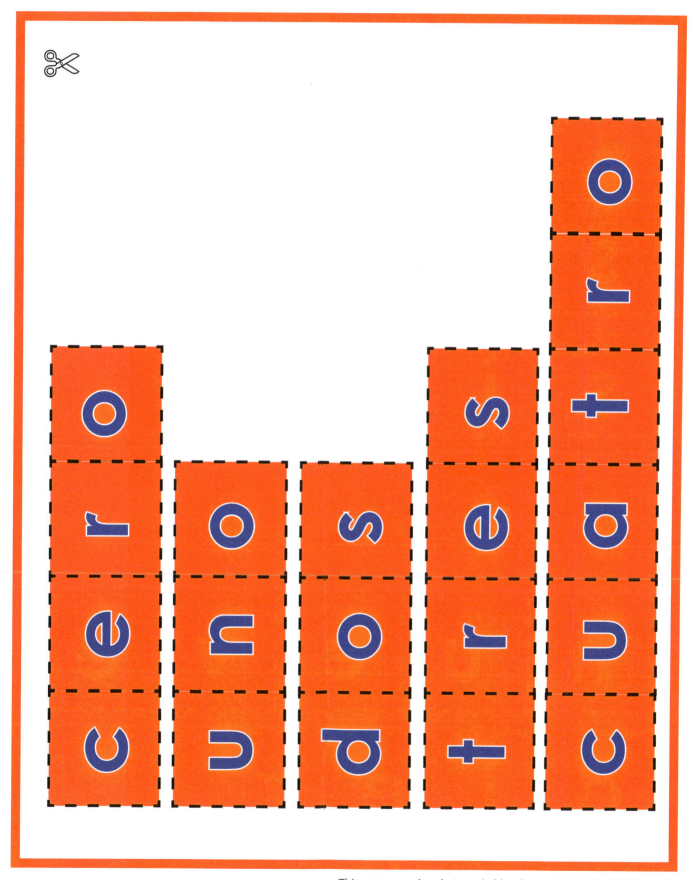

## Shuffle Up – Numbers

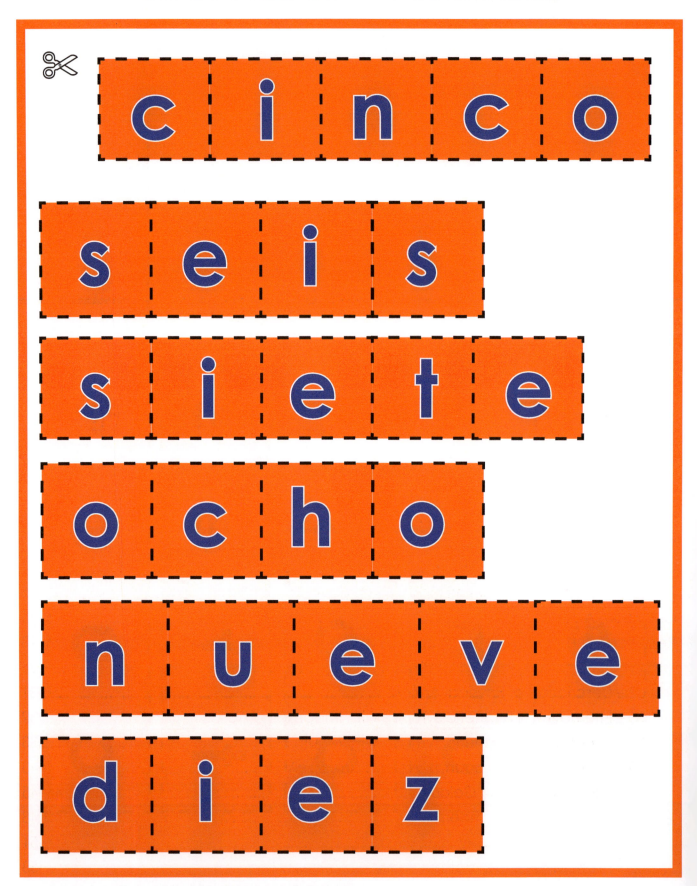

# Shuffle Up – Numbers

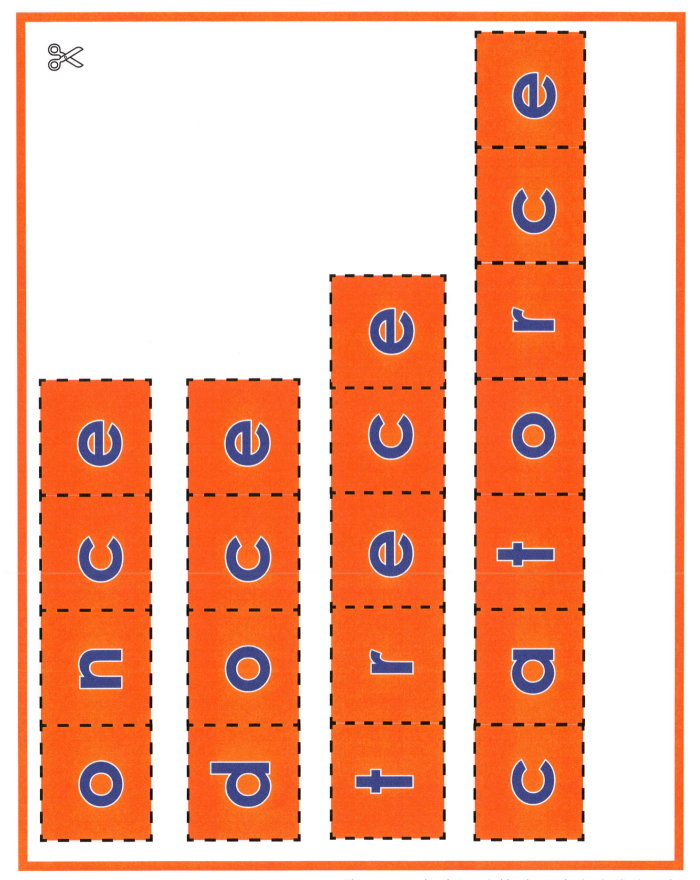

## Shuffle Up – Days of the Week

## Shuffle Up – Months of the Year

e | n | e | r | o

f | e | b

r | e | r | o

m | a | r | z | o

a | b | r | i | l

m | a | y | o

# Shuffle Up – Months of the Year

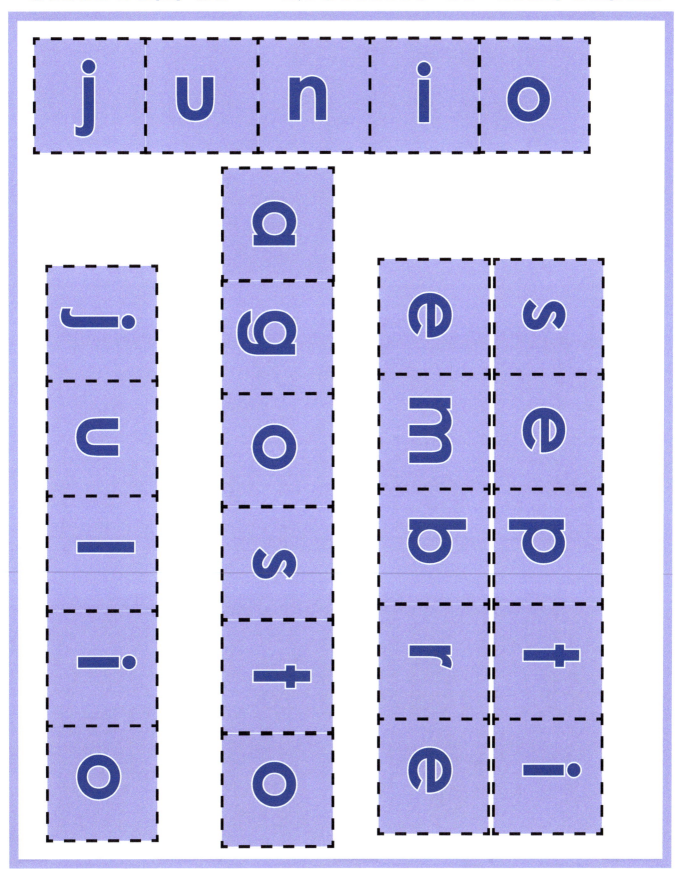

## Shuffle Up – Months of the Year

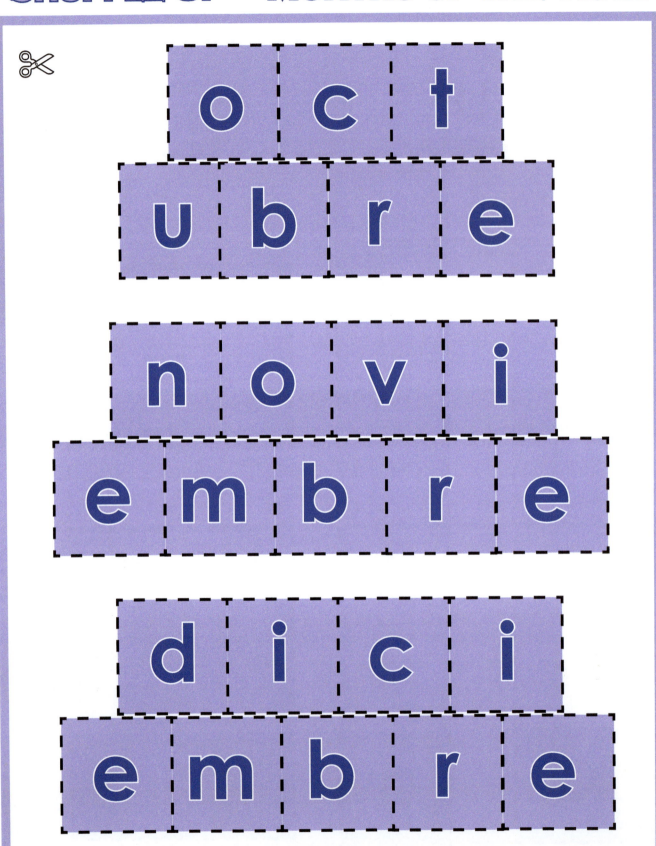

# Which Am I?

Choose 5 or 6 phonemes that you wish to practise. Give students the grapheme cards for these phonemes (using Resource R11, pages 57–61). Say a word which uses the phoneme and ask them to hold up the correct card(s). (Please note: depending on the sounds you choose to practise, children may hold up more than one grapheme for each word.)

| International Phonetic Symbol | Grapheme(s) | Sample Words |
|---|---|---|
| /a/ | a | bl**a**nco, g**a**to, p**a**dre, m**a**dre |
| /b/ | **b** at the beginning of a word | **b**ueno, **b**lanco |
| | **v** at the beginning of a word | **v**erde |
| | **b** after a nasal consonant | ha**m**burguesa |
| | **v** after a nasal consonant | in**v**ento |
| /β/ | **b** after a vowel | de**b**ate |
| | **v** after a vowel | nue**v**e |
| | **b** after a non-nasal consonant | ál**b**um |
| | **v** after a non-nasal consonant | reser**v**ar |
| /k/ | **c** before **a/o/u** | **c**apital, **c**o**c**odrilo, **c**ultura, blan**c**o, cin**c**o, **c**uatro |
| | k | **k**ilo |
| | **qu** before **e** or **i** | **qu**é, mos**qu**ito |
| /θ/ | **c** before **e** or **i** | **c**ero, **c**inco |
| | z | a**z**ul |
| /tʃ/ | ch | o**ch**o |
| /d/ | **d** at the beginning of a word | **d**ónde, **d**os, **d**iez |
| | **d** after a nasal consonant | in**d**icar |
| | **d** after l | fal**d**a |

# Which Am I?

| International Phonetic Symbol | Grapheme(s) | Sample Words |
|---|---|---|
| /ð/ | **d** after a vowel | me**d**ia, mora**d**o, pa**d**re, ma**d**re |
| | **d** after a non-nasal consonant, excluding **l** | sar**d**ina, ver**d**e |
| /e/ | **e** | tr**e**s, di**e**z, v**e**rd**e**, nu**e**v**e**, si**e**t**e** |
| /g/ | **g** before **a/o/u** | **g**ala, man**g**o, sin**g**ular |
| | **g** before a consonant | ne**g**ro, **g**ris |
| | **gu** before **e** or **i** | hambur**gu**esa, **gu**itarra |
| /x/ | **j** | ro**j**o, naran**j**a |
| | **g** before **e** or **i** | a**g**enda, **g**imnasio |
| /i/ | **i** | gr**i**s, amar**i**llo, c**i**nco, se**i**s, n**i**ño, n**i**ña |
| | **y** as a conjunction | **y** (and) |
| | **y** at the end of a word | ha**y**, re**y** |
| /j/ | **i** before a vowel, where it is not accented | s**i**ete |
| /ʝ/ | **ll** | amari**ll**o |
| | **y** except at the end of a word or as a conjunction | pla**y**a |
| /ɲ/ | **ñ** | ni**ñ**o, ni**ñ**a, ara**ñ**a |
| /o/ | **o** | blanc**o**, r**o**j**o** |
| /ɾ/ | **r** except at the beginning of a word, after **n/l/s** or before a consonant | mo**r**ado, amarillo, neg**r**o, g**r**is, naranja, ce**r**o, t**r**es, cuat**r**o, pad**r**e, mad**r**e |

# Which Am I?

| International Phonetic Symbol | Grapheme(s) | Sample Words |
|---|---|---|
| /r/ | r at the beginning of a word | rosa, rojo |
| | r after **n/l/s** | Enrique, alrededor, Israel |
| | r before a consonant | verde |
| | **rr** | marrón |
| /u/ | u | azul, uno |
| /w/ | ü | pingüino |
| | u before **a/e/o** | cuatro, nueve, antiguo, abuelo, abuela |